China

CHINA

Jonathan Bliss

The Rourke Corporation, Inc.

The Rourke Corporation, Inc.
P.O. Box 3328, Vero Beach, FL 32964

Bliss, Jonathan.
     China / Jonathan Bliss.
         p. cm. — (World partners)
     Includes bibliographical references and index.
     Summary: discusses China's present and future in a precarious time of sweeping economic reform, a time in which it possesses powerful nuclear technology, a time of unthinkable violence in which repression of the people is once again taking over.
     ISBN 0-86593-090-2
     1. China—Juvenile literature.   [1. China.]   I. Title.   II. Series.
DS706.B56   1990
951.05—dc20   90-8738
                                          CIP
                                          AC

Series Editor: Gregory Lee
Editors: Elizabeth Sirimarco and Marguerite Aronowitz
Book design and production: The Creative Spark, Capistrano Beach, CA
Cover photograph: Jeff foott/Tom Stack & Associates

China

Table of Contents

1 Understanding China

The Chinese have the oldest civilization on earth, going back some four thousand years. They have the oldest government ruled by a central authority, surviving with only minor interruptions since 221 B.C. China also has the largest population of any country in the world: more than 1.1 billion people. That's six times as many people as live in the United States, and half as many people as in the next most highly populated country in the world, India (800 million).

With a total land area of more than 3.7 million square miles, the People's Republic of China is the third largest country in the world (behind the Soviet Union and Canada), and is only slightly larger than the fourth largest country—the United States. As of 1987, China had 55 minority nationalities—including Tibetans—within its borders. While China recognizes one official language, Mandarin Chinese, there are more than one hundred Chinese *dialects* (distinct variations of the language) and other languages spoken there.

Traditionally poor because of its huge population, China in the 1980s was suddenly a nation on the move, rapidly modernizing as its leaders began sweeping economic reforms. Other

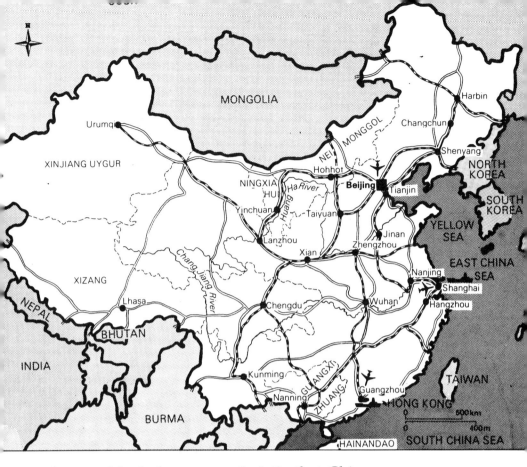

nations suddenly became optimistic that China would finally take its place as a valued world partner. Then, in 1989, the tragedy in Tiananmen Square occurred, and China lost much of its prestige and promise. This book will describe how it all happened: where China is today, how it got there, and where it may go from here.

China After Mao

The deaths of the two most important men in modern Chinese history occurred in 1976. In January, Zhou Enlai died. Highly intelligent, well-traveled and well-educated, Zhou had pushed for China to open up to the West. He was chiefly responsible for inviting President Richard Nixon to visit China, and had headed the movement to modernize his nation.

Then, in September 1976, the founder and spiritual leader of modern China, Mao Zedong, died at age 81. It was just 27 years after the official formation of the People's Republic of China. Mao had outlived almost every other member of the Long March, the legendary event that led to the Communist takeover of China. Although Mao had transformed China from a rigid monarchy to a Marxist state, he had failed to change the basic way things were done in China. Might was still right. The individual in China was still unimportant. People still had no more voice in the daily workings of their government than they had before. The peasants still starved.

To bring his movement to power and to keep it there, Mao attempted many economic and cultural plans during his 27 years in power, including a series of "Five-Year Plans," the "Great Leap Forward," and the "Cultural Revolution." His economic policies resulted in shortages of food and raw materials. His political policies crushed disagreement and encouraged sameness. Through a large military and secret police, Mao ordered the "purging" of "counter-revolutionary" elements in society, which meant he had people imprisoned or killed for disagreeing with his policies.

By his own admission Mao was no city planner or economist, yet he constantly overruled his advisors when they tried to straighten out China's economic mess. He launched a series of campaigns that only made the situation worse. His Great Leap Forward was an attempt to centralize farming in the country, that is, control of all agricultural life by the government, including "teaching" farmers how to grow crops according to socialist models. The peasants, already deprived of their individual land, were forced to work on collective farms they did not know or care about.

Meanwhile, the government used propaganda—false, "sugar-coated" information designed to deceive or reassure people. The peasants were told that hunger was a thing of the past. People were ordered into collective eating halls and told to eat as much as they liked. Little did they know that what they were eating so quickly was all the food there was.

The "Leap" was an utter disaster and resulted in widespread famine. More than 20 million people died of starvation! Mao reluctantly abandoned the policies of the "Leap" in 1959, gave up many of his powers to men better suited to managing the problems of the country, and went into semi-retirement.

The Cultural Revolution

But Mao could not stay out of government for long. He feared that many of his advisors were gaining power and prestige. As a result, Mao started the "Cultural Revolution" in 1966. This was supposed to be an attack on government bureaucracy by reacquainting people in the big cities with the hardships of the peasant workers. But something went terribly wrong. The Cultural Revolution rapidly turned into a reign of terror. Children were suddenly required to denounce their parents and teachers. Mobs of young people who called themselves The Red Guard swarmed through China, beating and killing anyone who displayed signs of "elitist" skills or knowledge. Books were burned, and schools and universities were destroyed. Scholars, intellectuals and artists were exiled or murdered. Ancient art and architecture were smashed. In the end, it became a virtual war on anyone who had education, learning or talent above that of the average man.

The Cultural Revolution did not accomplish what Mao had planned. Instead it created a generation of know-nothings: millions of young men and women without education or any code of belief. Although many Red Guards have since tried to educate themselves as adult students in night classes, an entire generation in the professions and sciences is missing in China. The most able specialists in China today often seem to be either very young or very old.

Because of Mao's policies, China changed completely in less than 30 years. All land became the property of the state, and factories and farms were run for and by the government. As in the Soviet Union, every adult was guaranteed a job, even though there was little choice about the job a person was given and no choice about the amount of wages received. The only way to get ahead was as a member of the Chinese Communist Party (CCP).

Most important, the long, rich history of China was "revised" to reflect the new government's dislike of China's former traditions, culture and values. Mao and his followers had erased nearly 40 centuries of dynastic history in less than three decades. But despite all these changes, the life of the average Chinese after Mao was no better than it had been a thousand years before.

The man who remained to rule over the post-Mao period was Deng Xiaoping, a quiet little man with a remarkable ability to survive the rapid changes in Chinese politics. Condemned during Mao's reign for various acts of counterrevolutionary activity, Deng managed to avoid death and exile at every turn. By 1978 he had grabbed the real power and quickly set out to strengthen his position by reforming the party organization.

Deng realized that the country was in deep trouble. From a military point of view, there was danger on every side. To the west and north

Chinese History

2500 B.C.—*An advanced civilization arises in the Huang He (Yellow River) Valley of northern China. This is the beginning of nearly 4,000 years of uninterrupted civilization.*

1700-1027 B.C.—*The first dynasty, Xia (Hsia), is formed with its capital at Anyang in Henan Province.*

1027-221 B.C.—*The Zhou dynasty, which lasted longer than any other. This period is often called the Golden Age of China.*

551-479 B.C.—*Confucius founds a school of thought, Confucianism, which is to dominate Chinese thought for the next 3,000 years.*

476-221 B.C.—*The Warring States period.*

221-207 B.C.—*Qin Shihuangdi founds the Qin (Ch'in) dynasty, which unifies China and gives China its name in Western languages (Ch'in becomes China).*

206 B.C.-220 A.D.—*Han Dynasty emerges with the capital at Chang'an. During this period, both paper and porcelain are invented.*

581-716—*Rise of the Sui Dynasty. Invention of gunpowder and the wheelbarrow.*

618-907—*Tang Dynasty, often regarded as the high-point of Chinese civilization. The golden age of literature and art.*

Chinese History

1839-42—The Opium War.

1893—Mao Zedong is born.

1898—Between June 11 and September 21, the Qing emperor, Guangxu (1875-1908), ordered a series of reforms aimed at sweeping social and institutional changes. This brief period is called The Hundred Day's Reform. With the help of the Empress Dowager, Ci Xi (1835- 1908), ultraconservatives overthrew Guangxu and reestablished traditional Manchu rule.

1915—Japan takes Manchuria. They will keep it until 1928 when a coalition of warlords and generals sweep north to retake it.

1931—Japan seizes Manchuria once again and sets up the state of Manchukuo with the deposed emperor, Puyi, as head of its puppet government. This time they keep it until 1945 when Japan is defeated. Hundreds of thousands of Chinese are killed before the province is retaken.

1949—On October 1, the People's Republic of China is formally established.

1966-76—The Cultural Revolution.

1976—Mao Zedong and Zhou Enlai both die. Deng Xiaoping assumes power after brief struggle.

1989—The massacre at Tiananmen Square.

lay the vast Soviet Union, another Communist country to be sure, but one that had been on hostile terms with China since the 1960s. More than 100,000 Soviet troops and tanks were camped on their common border. To the east lay the newly-awakening Pacific Rim countries like Japan, Taiwan and South Korea, all enemies of China. To the south lay India, a huge democracy, who had waged constant border disputes with China since the 1950s. In fact, only two countries—North Korea and Albania—could be called long-time Chinese allies.

Economically, China was also in bad shape. Isolated for 30 years from the rest of the world, the Chinese economy had declined since the Communist takeover. There was a chronic shortage of almost everything except people. What goods were available were poorly made, and farming practices were too primitive to feed a billion people.

Deng's solution to the problem was to restore domestic calm, assure the people that the violence was over, institute real Communist Party reforms, and adopt a more liberal approach to business. This meant opening up China's markets to foreign investment, and trading Chinese goods on the international market. It turned out to be an excellent move.

Within 10 years, China had become a vigorous economic force, supplying many goods to a world market that appreciated the low prices China could deliver. The plight of the average Chinese improved considerably during the period from 1975 to 1989. A limited number of cars and televisions became available. More food appeared in the markets. Independent businesses sprang up, encouraged by Deng's economic policies. The average income jumped several hundred percent. Education became more liberal, and many Chinese students were allowed to study overseas in the hope they would return with knowledge of new technologies.

The United States was one of the first countries to welcome China back into the community of world nations. Japan and Europe also made gestures of friendship that included substantial investment in the country.

China's isolation was ending. Many people began predicting that with their population and industrial will, China would eventually challenge Japan and the United States for the role of economic world leader. There seemed little doubt that China would soon become a valuable world partner.

No one could predict what was to come.

2 Business And Industry In China

For at least 3,000 years, caravans have traveled to China in search of silks, spices, perfumes, teas, rugs, and a thousand other goods found only in that distant land. Early travelers returned from China speaking of a culture completely different from the primitive tribes that populated most of Europe and the rest of the world. They had never seen a civilization so advanced or refined.

The early success of China was due to many things. The Chinese had a written language at a time when many languages were only spoken. They had advanced technology, political institutions, highly refined arts, a creative intellectual life, and a large population.

The world came to China, and China did business with the world as it saw fit. Few Chinese felt a need to travel. They viewed the world outside China as barbarian and unpleasant. The Chinese felt safe in their cultural and technological superiority.

That sense of superiority lasted long enough for China to fall behind. While the world around China was changing, China stayed the same. While the world got richer and more technologically sophisticated, China looked inward and clung to the past. It was a Chinese scientist

who first discovered gunpowder in the 6th century, but it was European nations like England and Portugal who used gunpowder to subdue the Chinese and gain a foothold in China in the 18th century.

Chinese junks (flat-bottomed sailboats) carry goods down the Yangtze River.

By the mid-1700s, Europeans were no longer impressed by China. The foreign invaders had no awe of China's long, rich history. They saw only that it was a very poor, very backward country, ripe for the taking. So they took it.

For more than 150 years—from 1750 to 1900—the Chinese were thoroughly exploited by the West. Cities like Shanghai, Hong Kong, Macao and Canton became bustling ports for foreign trade, filled with European buildings and reflecting a European way of life. Industry sprang up in the larger cities. Smokestacks belched smoke, factory workers toiled, and bicycles and automobiles jammed ancient cobblestone streets. The modern world had come to China.

Production grew substantially between 1800 and 1949, and even increased after the Communist takeover. Before the 1980s, however, economic gains were largely matched by population growth, so that the economy barely kept up. There was never enough food to put away as a hedge against possible disaster, and disaster—like famine, flood and disease—was all too common.

Business Under Communism

Under China's socialist system, China had been able to greatly increase the amount of products it manufactured. While some industries were able to keep up with Western technology, most were not. In general, equipment produced by Chinese factories was years behind standard Western designs. For example, Chinese television sets, automobiles and farm equipment were of generally poor quality. Items like computers and sophisticated medical equipment were simply not made at all.

Mao and many of his followers believed that politics was more important than economics in the life of China. Mao was more concerned with raising the people's political consciousness than he was in making better cars or growing more wheat and rice. His attempts at improving the economy ended in failure. Other members of his party, such as Zhou Enlai and Deng Xiaoping, disagreed with Mao. But as long as Mao lived, his policies prevailed.

After Mao's death, the job of modernizing China was left to Deng, who believed that business was at least as important as politics. By 1977

Deng had taken up the modernization program that Zhou Enlai had started. His plan, called the *Four Modernizations*, stressed economic progress above the Maoist goals of class struggle and permanent revolution. The program called for modernizing agriculture, industry, science and technology. Profit incentives and bonuses took the place of political slogans and red banners, as China's leaders experimented with ways to get the economy going.

Deng's first step was to loosen government controls on many businesses. The government had been controlling all aspects of China's economy for 30 years, and things were getting worse, not better, for the average Chinese family.

Slowly, Deng began to remove the controls and set the market free. Peasant households were given greater control over what was grown and how it was sold. Farm families were allowed

China's undisputed leader is Deng Xiaoping, yet he holds no official government post. His leadership has been a curious balance of economic reforms and continued repression of political dissent.

to lease land and grow crops of their own choosing. Private enterprise and free markets were opened up. Profit incentives were provided for workers in factories.

By the mid-1980s, industrial and agricultural reforms had achieved success in some areas. Industrial output in 1986 was about 25 times that of 1952. A wide range of industries had been established, and the country was one of the world's leaders in coal, textiles and bicycle production. There were major plants in almost every key industry, and a strong effort had been made to introduce manufacturing into undeveloped and rural areas.

Despite the progress, major problems remained. Most large manufacturing operations continued to be slowed by inefficient equipment. Energy problems grew worse. Despite large deposits of coal and many hydroelectric plants, China could not generate enough electricity needed for its economy.

Faced with mounting problems, Deng introduced a dramatic new policy in the late 1980s. Foreign business was invited in, and foreign governments were encouraged to invest. China opened its doors wide to the world. To symbolize this change of heart, most government officials took off their "Mao jackets" and put on Western-style ties and coats.

The result was a sudden surge of business activity. Supermarkets and department stores filled with consumer goods from America, Japan and China began springing up in the major cities.

Farming

Despite a huge population, only 10 percent of China is actually under cultivation. Most of this land is in the eastern third of the country where most of the population lives. The 90 per-

cent that remains is either mountains, desert or urban areas.

Wheat has traditionally been the main crop in northern China, and rice is the main grain crop in the south. Other crops include millet, barley, cotton, corn, sorghum, soybeans, peanuts and tea. Through the use of fertilizers and irrigation, much of the cultivated land supports high yields. In the south where the growing season is long, two or even three crops a year can be grown on the same land.

Since the beginning of the Four Modernizations, China has expanded and updated its agricultural methods. New strains of rice and wheat are being tried, and communal farming is giving way to private farming.

Much of the agriculture in China is still done through communes. Hundreds of people work for a particular commune farm. Within each commune, workers are divided into work groups called *brigades*. Each worker must work a certain number of hours each day for the brigade, even if he or she must also attend to a private plot of land.

The new agricultural policies have also increased the number of outlets for food and other products within China. From 1978 to 1985 the number of food stores rose from 33,000 to 61,000. Household income rose dramatically over the same period, from Y134 ($36) per year in 1978 to Y397 ($107) in 1985 ("Y" = *yen*, Chinese money). Income inequality also increased. The end of many collective factories and farms brought decreases in health, education and welfare services for the rural population.

In the late 1980s, China was ready to confront growing demands for higher agricultural production. However, the size and diversity of the country—in both geography and population—presented a real challenge.

To begin with, there is never enough of anything. What land can be cultivated is still plowed and prepared in the old way—by hand and foot—using enormous numbers of laborers for planting and harvesting. Such labor-saving devices as tractors, bulldozers and harvesters are either non-existent or in short supply. Technology could greatly increase the land's yield, but it would also put millions of laborers out of work. This presents a problem for the government: should it attempt to update its equipment in order to produce more, or should it continue to guarantee full employment of its massive work force at the expense of its future? Either way, it cannot win.

Industry

Most heavy industry in China is concentrated in the large coastal cities and in the northeast. Shanghai is the largest industrial center, followed by Anshan, Fushun and Shenyang. Like agriculture, industry has enjoyed the changes that have occurred in China.

Urban dwellers have experienced an increase in their standard of living. Citizens started buying television sets, radios, and even VCRs. Housing improved as more citizens were able to pay for improvements in their standard of living.

As things became better in China, foreign companies felt better about investing there. The World Bank alone helped finance 59 projects in China to the tune of $7 billion. Foreign investment, especially from Europe, Japan and the United States, increased many times between the years 1985 and 1989.

In 1986, the government recognized four kinds of economic enterprise in China: ownership by the people (or state ownership), collective, individual, and other. Most of the largest industries in China are still state-owned and

Facts and Figures

• As of April 15, 1989, the population of China was 1.1 billion—nearly five times that of the United States.

• The most crowded city is Guangzhou (Canton). During one week in February, 1989, 1 million people migrated to the city looking for jobs.

• 23,000 couples marry in China each day.

• "Marry late, have one child," read billboards all over China. This is part of the government's attempt to discourage overpopulation.

• Peasants who grow rice earn five times the salary of a university professor.

• 7,000 varieties of rice ("fan") are grown in China.

• It takes 1,000 silkworm cocoons to make a single blouse.

• 70 tons of dirt and soot from coal and diesel exhaust fall on Shanghai every day.

state-run. Some are well run, others are not. Chief among the obstacles to high production in state-owned enterprises are the "iron rice bowls"—jobs handed down from parent to child, from relative to relative, in what is known as the *dingti* system. These jobs are given not on the basis of merit or enthusiasm, but rather on the basis of family connections. Since these jobs are guaranteed, the worker feels little pressure to work hard. The job will still be there whether workers produce one car a day or ten.

The second level of enterprise after state-owned is the collective. Some of the oldest, most worn-out machinery in China can be found in collective factories, but they are also places where you can often find the most ingenuity and enthusiasm. In the beginning, collective factories were merely branch factories of state enterprises formed to give employment to people who had not been provided for by *dingti*. But their role and objective changed. By 1981 there were more than 13 million townspeople working in collectives, and their numbers were growing rapidly. Average wages in collectives are only three-quarters of those paid in state-owned enterprises, and most collectives offer no welfare benefits. About five percent of the rural labor force works in nearly one-half million small-scale collectives that are owned by brigades, communes and country towns, instead of the state. With an average of about 30 workers per collective, jobs in these businesses are much sought after. Wages are low compared to state factory jobs, but high compared to farming jobs.

There are also a relatively small but growing number of self-employed Chinese. According to official statistics, there were as few as 150,000 in 1978; however, by 1981, there had been a six-fold increase to 1.1 million self-employed people. By 1988 the number was much higher as shop-keepers, street peddlers, even independent businessmen began to appear in China's largest cities.

This leaves a group of people the government only refers to as "other," people who comprise the black market and non-conformists of Chinese life. As in Russia, the Chinese government has created many shortages in goods and services that enterprising (some would say outlaw) Chinese have taken advantage of. For exam-

The familiar skyline of Hong Kong: will this business mecca be absorbed by Communist China?

ple, on the black market you can buy goods that are difficult to find elsewhere, but you must pay high prices for them.

Despite the growing number of collectives, private businesses and self-employed people, prosperity and free market capitalism are still the exception rather than the rule.

Although China is the fourth largest producer of fuel, energy shortages remain a major obstacle to industrial growth. Waste is considerable, and the use of coal—accounting for 70 percent of all fuel consumption—produces staggering pollution. Proven oil reserves in 1985 were 700 billion tons, and estimated reserves were

3,000 billion tons. China had the world's sixth largest electric power-generating potential, but output still fell short of demand.

Although more independent, many industries still suffer from obsolete equipment and poor management techniques. For example, there are about 120 major enterprises that produce most of China's machine tools. Yet overall, the machine tool industry is based on 1960s technology. The automotive industry, which grew substantially after 1949, did not keep pace with the demands of modernization. By 1985, tough government measures had limited imports, and the country's own automakers were not able to produce more than a few hundred thousand cars a year.

High tech industry came to China in the limited form of disk drive parts, computer chips and new laser assemblies, but without the means of developing new technology.

Aircraft assembly began in Shanghai during the early 1980s and has flourished. By 1987 China had become the world's fifth largest producer of iron and steel, even though it lagged far behind developed countries in production methods and quality. Reserves of gold, tungsten and various rare earth metals were being mined in large quantities. Production of television sets, radios, tape recorders and washing machines increased tenfold from 1976 to 1986. Many other industries such as chemicals, papermaking, food processing and mining increased output substantially. Even China's fish output increased, reaching 10 million tons by 1988.

The Economy Today

One of the truly bright spots for business in China today is the textile business. Textiles experienced such a rapid expansion during the

1980s that by 1989 many European countries were actively supporting a pact to restrict importation of Chinese carpets, silk fabrics and clothing. Such goods can be made more cheaply in China than almost anywhere else.

Despite their great progress under Deng's Four Modernizations program, however, most businesses still have problems. There is a need for newer equipment, higher quality goods, more open markets, more profit, and—as always— more goods and services. State factories cannot compete, yet there are more of them than any other kind of factory. The Chinese economy is still dominated by government regulation and planning, although more and more the government has had to let market forces determine prices and products. The rising and falling of prices for goods and services has resulted in inflation. In 1985, the increase in the prices of goods and services was 11.9 percent; by 1986, the figure had dropped to 7.6 percent. These are higher figures than are found in Japan or the United States, but much lower than other third-world countries like Brazil or Argentina.

It is obvious that many people—especially city dwellers—are better off today than they have been for a long time. There are more goods available to buy, more money with which to buy them, and a greater optimism about China's future. By 1989, workers throughout the country were beginning to believe that China might become the world power that their government had always assured them they already were.

3 Science, Education And Health Care

As with so much else in China, the development of science and technology has been difficult. Both have suffered frequent setbacks under the policies of Mao and his followers. The large and poorly educated rural population and the limited opportunities for secondary and college education are partially to blame. And resources seem to be available to only a few scientists, like those in the military.

China once led the world in scientific and technological innovation. Papermaking was invented here, along with ink, silk, and the first rockets. The water-powered mill, iron-casting, porcelain, and one of the world's first accurate calendars were all Chinese inventions. The first systematic studies of the human body and the heavens were done in China.

But in the 12th and 13th centuries, China seemed to stop caring about science and technology. By the middle of the 20th century, the nation had allowed itself to sink into hopeless ignorance of the modern world. Only in the last 30 years have science and technology become important again.

Since the Communist takeover, China's leaders involved themselves in policies regarding science to a greater extent than have leaders

of other countries. This would have been okay if these leaders knew anything about science, but unfortunately they usually have been as scientifically illiterate as most other world leaders. In an attempt to control the sciences without knowing what they were doing, China's leaders ended up hindering development.

Tension between scientists and Chinese leaders has existed since the earliest days of the People's Republic. For a while in the 1950s, the Soviet model was adopted by the Chinese. Administrators, not scientists, controlled projects. Individual scientists were seen as skilled employees expected to work as quietly and efficiently as the parts in a perfect machine. Scientific information was tightly controlled and flowed only through authorized channels. During the Cultural Revolution, a scientist could

Agricultural experimentation with new rice and wheat strains is explained to this group on a farm in Ningxia. Feeding China's enormous population is one of the most formidable problems facing Chinese leaders.

be imprisoned or killed merely for what he knew.

In the early 1970s, Deng Xiaoping and Zhou Enlai tried to improve the lot of scientists by separating the study of science from the study of politics. In 1975, Deng's Four Modernizations called for immediate deregulation of the sciences. Deng became the champion of Chinese science and technology.

By the early 1980s, substantial progress had been made to bring Chinese science and technology up to date. More funds were found for scientific institutions and students were encouraged to study science in schools and universities. Promising students were given scholarships and visas to study in places like the United States, Japan and Europe. The Chinese media devoted much attention to the value of science.

But by 1989, China still suffered from an acute shortage of scientists, technicians and engineers. The Cultural Revolution had removed an entire generation from education and professional training, creating a huge gap in the scientific work force.

Still there are some important signs of change in China and some successes. Thousands of miles of electrical and telephone wire have been laid down, millions of new phones have been installed, satellite service has begun, and such modern conveniences as the FAX machine, computers and modems have appeared, especially in cities like Shanghai and Beijing.

Television has become more common in China, available to more people than before. This has not only spread the government's message of reform, but has created expectations of change in the minds of many citizens.

Foreign investment has encouraged the development of a fledgling computer industry. While Chinese scientists still lack the means of developing new technologies, they have worked with Japanese and American firms to create factories that could assemble computer components. However, fundamental problems still remain for the computer business in China. Because of the complexity of Chinese script, for example, it is difficult to design keyboards or write computer programs for the Chinese scientific market. Programs are often written in English or a form of Chinese using the Roman alphabet.

Chinese scientists have also become far more visible and vocal in the areas of ecology as they criticize the rampant pollution and destruction of China's land, air and water. The last 30 years have not been kind to China's forests or wildlife. Many species are dangerously near extinction, including China's symbol, the Giant Panda. Parts of China that were once dense forest are now wasteland that is quickly turning to desert because of overpopulation, poor farming techniques, and a simple disregard for the environment. In cities like Beijing and Shanghai, the air is always thick with pollutants.

If science and technology is the key to the future, then China will have a very bleak future indeed. The nation now faces difficult problems in every facet of science and technology. It has few scientists to do much-needed research and few advanced technologies to develop the research that is done. Inevitably, China can only fall further behind. Without the advanced technologies it will take to solve their worsening problems, the problems will eventually turn into disasters.

One of the most important assets of old China was its educational system. For almost 2,000 years, education was the one sure way of getting work in the Chinese system. Through a rigorous examination system, students entered government civil service where they could rise as far and as fast as they were able. Therefore, education was linked to success, possible wealth, and certainly an increase in family status.

Many top government officials often started out as humble country students who had done well in the formal examinations and received government positions. However, only men could be civil servants; schools were open to boys only. Some girls were taught to read and write by their fathers but, for the most part, an educated woman was looked on with suspicion and avoided by prospective husbands. A popular proverb of the day was, "a woman with education causes trouble." Most men were looking for a woman with good manners, family connections, and bound feet.

All this changed dramatically under Mao. The old examination system was abolished. New subjects studied consisted largely of readings from Mao, Marx and Lenin. Colleges and universities were abandoned in favor of self-criticism sessions, political indoctrination seminars, and political awareness lectures.

Education

From the earliest times, Chinese education consisted of reading, writing, and memorizing the classics. Boys might be made to learn a passage of a thousand characters whose meaning was not explained. When a student was judged to know all the words and able to repeat them, he had to turn away from the book and repeat the text, first as it was written, then backwards. At every mistake the teacher, cane in hand, might hit him. This was known as the *bei shu* (back to the book) system.

Both moral instruction and strict memorizing still play a large part in Chinese education, especially at the primary and secondary school

levels. School children are encouraged to display the same kind of cooperation they show at home. Aggression, individualism and competitiveness are discouraged. A primary school will put up public lists showing good deeds done by different children as well as their marks in class.

Primary schools take children from ages six to 12. Here they are taught elementary mathematics, basic use of the abacus, reading and writing. All subjects involve a lot of memorizing. The government has a long-term policy of teaching everyone in the country *putonghua*, the Mandarin dialect, even though in most areas of China it has to be learned as a second language.

It isn't until junior-middle school, which takes pupils from ages 12 to 16, that a first foreign language—usually English—is taught. In most senior-middle schools (from ages 16 to 18), there is no other language available. The average

▲
China's largest resource is its enormous population— over one billion people. Keeping rural children healthy through vaccination, therefore, is no small task.

middle school year has two semesters, totaling nine months. School days are eight to ten hours long. The academic curriculum includes Chinese (Mandarin), mathematics, physics, chemistry, geology, history, geography, politics, music, fine arts, and physical education. Some middle schools also offer vocational training.

Literacy in China is about 75 percent and growing steadily. Ten percent of primary school pupils and 25 percent of junior-middle school children leave school, mainly to work. Only one child in three goes on to senior-middle school. Of this number, less than 50 percent will go on to college.

Since 1986, policy-makers have established a compulsory nine-year law. This means that every boy and girl in China must now attend school at least nine years, or through junior-middle school. This new policy is designed to increase the amount of time students, especially rural students, spend in the classroom. Before this plan went into effect, the average rural student spent only four to six years in school before going off to work.

The goal of most children in China is to attend a university or college. Yet the quality of college education has not always been high, and chances of getting accepted are not good for most children. The government now offers financial help in the way of scholarships and grants to students from rural areas, and there has been considerable interest in television, radio, and correspondence classes to supplement regular college enrollment.

China has also reformed faculty appointment practices. By 1989, colleges and universities had the freedom to choose their own teachers.

Despite advances in higher education, China still lags behind other countries in the quality of its education. For this reason, many of

China Today

- In addition to written exams, most university applicants must pass a physical exam and a political screening.

- The average pair of shoes in Wenzhou is $8.

- Only one-tenth of China's land is used to grow crops.

- Once green, northern China has turned into a desert because of unchecked woodcutting.

- Pants with "rear windows" are available for infants and toddlers since diapers are unheard of in China.

- Some high school students receive military training. A network of people's militia augments the police force and the People's Liberation Army.

- The tobacco capital of China is Yongding District in Fujian Province. More land is set aside for yan cao ("smokeweed") than for tea.

- The most common last name in China is ma or "horse."

- Most Chinese would consider themselves fortunate to own their own bicycle. The state continues to control the annual production of new bicycles so that anyone who wishes to buy one must first obtain permission from his collective or factory.

- The Baoshan General Iron and Steel Works in Shanghai is one of the most important enterprises in China.

China's most promising students are now given the opportunity to study abroad. In most cases, the government pays for tuition, room and board while the students are away. Although figures vary, some 36,000 students studied in 14 countries between 1978 and 1984. As of 1986, there were 15,000 Chinese scholars and students in American universities alone, compared with a total of 19,000 scholars sent abroad between 1979 and 1983. Chinese academic exchanges with the West and Japan are common today.

Teachers and scholars are still poorly paid, however, and students continue to have only a limited choice of subjects and schooling to choose from. Intellectuals and college students in general are viewed suspiciously by the current government.

Health Care

Health care today in China offers both traditional Chinese and modern Western medical treatment. The Chinese regard health as a state of balance established between the body and the natural world around it. Those illnesses caused by heat, overeating or "overfullness" are called *yang* diseases. Those diseases caused by cold or deficiency are called *yin* diseases. The task of the traditional caregiver, therefore, is to keep the yin and yang elements in balance.

The human body is thought of as a system containing vital energy, or *qi*. The traditional Chinese doctor's job is to intervene with the body's function through the use of drugs or herbs or through the manipulation of the skin. This manipulation means *acupuncture, moxibustion*, and *acupressure*—the use of needles, burning fibers or pressure—to block or unblock the flow of *qi* through the body.

At one time Western medicine scoffed at

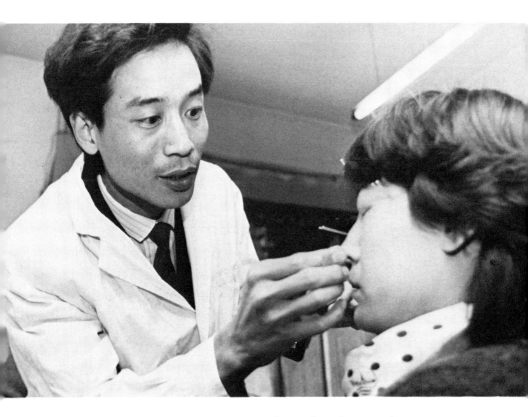

Chinese remedies but, more recently, it has been shown that many of these methods for relieving pain or curing disease are very effective. Acupuncture is now being used as a local anesthetic in many parts of the world, including Europe and the United States.

On the streets of China, peddlers and stall-keepers still sell herbal compounds much as they did a thousand years ago. Fifty or 60 different varieties are on display, ranging from plant bulbs for curing rheumatoid arthritis to rhinoceros horn for a variety of ailments. Perhaps the best known of these herbs is the ginseng root, which is supposed to strengthen the entire system and lengthen life span.

China also has a tradition of using massage and gymnastics to strengthen the body. Every morning in every city and town throughout China, men and women gather in public

An acupuncturist inserts needles under the skin of a patient. Acupuncture is a drug-free method of relieving pain that has generated much interest among western medical researchers.

parks to do exercises like *tai-chi*.

In the early 20th century, many thinkers in China rejected traditional Chinese medicines and methods. Sun Yat-sen, the founding father of the old Republic of China and a doctor trained in the West, helped introduce modern medicine to China. Although modern medicine was slow to catch on, Western-style methods are used today to cure and prevent many diseases.

The Chinese government has also used modern medical techniques to greatly improve the country's sanitation and hygiene. Beginning in 1950, the government launched campaigns to get rid of pests such as rats, flies and mosquitoes. Efforts were made to improve water quality, and waste disposal plants were built in the cities to take care of sewage. As a result, such epidemic diseases as cholera, plague, typhoid and scarlet fever have been almost eliminated.

The government has also greatly increased the number and quality of health care personnel. In 1949 there were 33,000 nurses and 363,000 physicians in the country; by 1985 the numbers had risen to 637,000 nurses and 1.4 million physicians.

China continues to face serious problems, however, in keeping its citizens healthy. Epidemics still kill thousands, and many of China's doctors must be trained overseas because Chinese medical schools are so inadequate. The availability and quality of health care varies widely from region to region.

The major medical problem facing China today is overpopulation. One-quarter of all human beings on this planet are Chinese. The average density of the country is approximately 300 people for every square mile.

While families in the cities are growing smaller, farming families still produce large

numbers of children. The government has done what it could to discourage child-bearing, including passing laws to restrict families to one child. But large families continue to exist, representing a problem that can only get worse. Between 1975 and 1988, China added another 100 million citizens, for a yearly population increase of 1.4 percent. If this trend continues, the population of China will exceed 1.2 billion people by the year 2000.

On a Shanghai morning young and old alike turn out to perform their Tai Chi Chuan *exercises in the park.*

4 Military And Defense

China has a long military tradition dating back to the earliest days of recorded history. Dynasties rose and fell as a result of warfare. The most successful warriors often became emperors. Both Mongol and Manchu tribes from Central Asia conquered China and formed dynastic orders. It was always military might that decided who would rule China and for how long.

The modern People's Republic is no less an example of military might. Mao came to power because of his peasant army. Later, Mao kept power and enforced his will using the army. Even today, few men in China can afford to rule without the help of the People's Liberation Army (PLA). Mao himself once said that "truth comes from the barrel of a gun." This, unfortunately, has proven to be all too correct in modern Chinese history.

China's government, as with many other nations, spends large sums on the military—Y20.4 billion or $5.5 billion in 1987. By the late 1980s, the PLA forces consisted of various arms of the ground forces: the Air Force, the Navy, and the Strategic Missile Force (also known as the Second Artillery Corps).

All of these branches face serious prob-

lems. For one thing, many of the weapons used by the military are either obsolete or of poor quality. Another problem is the way Chinese civilians now view the military. Starting in the late 1970s, the Chinese people have felt a growing resentment toward the military. A traditional saying is, "one doesn't make nails out of good iron; one doesn't make soldiers out of good men." To restore a damaged image, the government started in the late 1980s to praise the PLA's virtues in the media, including the great strides made in military modernization.

Despite these problems, more than three million Chinese are in uniform today, representing the largest military force in the world. Technological improvement has meant greater sophistication for the Chinese military, who can now boast a modern Air Force and a lethal arsenal of rockets, tanks and automatic arms. Despite

A drill unit from the Chinese People's Liberation Army.

Cultural Policies

The policy of Four Modernizations helped create a period of artistic and cultural freedom in China. After the oppression of the Cultural Revolution that saw the closing of most theaters and museums, China began to recover.

Traditional Chinese opera now flourishes in the cities. The Beijing Opera continues to be very popular, and Western drama is performed by an ever-increasing number of theatrical troupes. Music, both traditional Chinese and Western, has discovered a new voice since the end of the Cultural Revolution. Painting, sculpture and calligraphy are now taught in many colleges and universities. The number of artists practicing these crafts has increased since the beginning of the Four Modernizations.

Motion pictures, television and radio, which used to be used exclusively for propaganda, can now produce and present a greater variety of subjects. It is estimated that 85 percent of the urban population has access to television.

Publishing is once again tolerated—if not openly encouraged—after years of censorship. While a book, magazine, or newspaper must still watch what it says, it is becoming increasingly more acceptable for writers to address the topics they really want to write about. This openness reached new levels during 1988 and 1989, when newspapers and magazines began publishing articles that were openly critical of China's government and demanded greater democratic freedom.

With more economic freedom has come greater cultural and artistic exchange with the West. For the first time, Chinese athletes recently began appearing in international competitions, such as the Olympics. They show particular prowess in such sports as ping-pong, gymnastics and diving.

this, the military remains a land-based operation designed to protect borders and safeguard its leaders.

China has also become a large seller of weapons to foreign countries, some of which are very sophisticated. For example, the Chinese Silkworm shore-to-ship missile has become part of many countries' military stockpiles. So has the Dongfeng-3 intermediate-range missile. The Silkworm was used by Iran to damage an American ship in the Persian Gulf, and the Dongfeng-3 was recently sold to Saudi Arabia.

What makes China dangerous in an international context is its possession of nuclear weapons. By the late 1980s, China was the world's third-largest nuclear power, having in its possession between 225 and 300 nuclear weapons. Both hydrogen and atomic bombs are stockpiled in China's arsenal, along with the rockets needed to transport those bombs to foreign lands. This makes China a major threat to world peace.

Since 1960, China has considered the Soviet Union its main threat to security. Lesser threats are posed by long-standing border disputes with Vietnam and India. Ongoing troubles in Tibet also require the PLA's constant supervision. It is estimated that more than 100,000 Tibetans have been killed by the Chinese military since China took over Tibet (now called the Xizang Autonomous Region) in 1950.

The Aftermath Of Tiananmen Square

In the last 12 years, China has experienced the most sustained period of economic and cultural growth in its history. Greater economic freedom made for a more prosperous nation, and prosperity in turn meant a higher standard of living for many of China's citizens. When people live better, they feel better about themselves and their country. There is greater optimism and hope among the Chinese about their future than ever before. Under Deng's rule, China has enjoyed more international goodwill. Moreover, as China developed into a world partner, a free exchange of ideas emerged. More and more Chinese students went abroad to learn technical skills, and returned with those skills to teach others. Universities were thriving. New ideas like democracy and capitalism were being discussed on college campuses.

For the first time newspapers and magazines could openly criticize the government. Many abuses of power that had always been ignored were uncovered. People began to notice that government officials and their relatives lived considerably better than the rest of the population. Sons and relatives of government officials were always the first ones to get good government jobs. An elite group of bureaucrats in

Beijing and other major cities had their own cars, spacious houses, expensive trips abroad, and private stores. Yet many people in the countryside starved. This inequality helped to ignite the protest that became the Tiananmen Square disaster.

It began in May 1989 as a tribute to Hu Yaobang, former head of the Chinese Communist Party, and grew into a protest against Deng's government. In the beginning, most of the protesters were students from local universities. They gathered in Beijing's giant Tiananmen Square to observe Hu's death, chant slogans, and argue the merits of reform. Over the course of the next two weeks, the protests became larger as more and more people joined in. The Square began to fill up.

In late May, Mikhail Gorbachev, premier of the Soviet Union, made an historic visit to Beijing. It represented the first time in more than

More than 100,000 people—mostly young students—crowded Tiananmen Square daily in the spring of 1989 to urge China's leaders to accept democratic reforms.

25 years that a Soviet leader had visited China. Deng Xiaoping welcomed Gorbachev with enthusiasm and banquets in the Great Hall of the People. No doubt Deng hoped that such a gesture by the Soviet Union would signal a new era of peace and cooperation between the two communist countries. He could not, however, foresee the impact that Gorbachev's visit would have on the students in Tiananmen Square.

Gorbachev had become an international celebrity, a symbol of liberation throughout the world. Wherever he visited oppressed countries, it seemed that new freedoms soon followed. Certainly the students believed this, for his visit increased their calls for democracy in China.

The number of people in the Square increased fourfold over the two days Gorbachev was in China, and continued to grow even after he left. Suddenly it wasn't just students who were marching for freedom, but workers and peasants. A tent city sprang up in the Square, and several hundred students began a hunger strike.

The international press that was covering Gorbachev's summit could not ignore what was going on in the streets. Before long the celebrations in the Great Hall of the People were overshadowed completely by the protests in Tiananmen Square. The world began to watch as Chinese students waved flags and marched, their fingers raised in the "V" sign for victory. But the government remained silent and did nothing.

The Chinese leaders were arguing among themselves. As the protest spread beyond the Square to Beijing and other cities like Shanghai and Nanchang, the men in power took sides. On the students' side emerged Zhao Ziyang, the party general secretary, who agreed with the students that greater openness was needed and that more democracy was a good thing. On the other side were conservatives like Li Peng and President Yang Shang-kun. The man who made the difference, Deng Xiaoping, waited for several days, watching the protest build and calculating his strength.

At last the government moved. The students were ordered to leave the Square. When the protesters refused, the army sent in troops to "calm" the disturbance. But these troops, mostly young men from the country, did not make it to the Square. They were intercepted on the outskirts of Beijing by crowds of people chanting and singing. Many of the soldiers actually joined the protest, along with large numbers of police. The rest of the army forces retreated from the barricades and crowds.

There had been no violence, and no one thought there would be. After all, Deng was a liberal, the man who had brought new hope and prosperity to China. Surely the man who had made protest possible would not be the one to stop it. The international press reported on the events with optimism. Democracy was breaking out all over in Eastern Europe, and it seemed that no country could be immune for long. Besides, the People's Army would not fire on the people. It was unthinkable.

But on the night of June 3, 1989, the unthinkable happened. The government—with Deng's blessing—ordered the 27th Army into Beijing. This time there was no conversation with the protesters. The troops opened fire with machine guns and rifles. Tanks rumbled forward, spraying bullets as they went, crushing protesters under their tracks. More troops, with bayonets fixed, charged into the square, firing into the crowd. While many in the crowd ran, many more stood their ground and waited for certain death. It was not long in coming.

When it was all over, more than one thou-

Tanks of the People's Liberation Army rolled into Beijing to squash the freedom demonstrations in Tiananmen Square. The resulting bloodshed— Chinese killing Chinese—shocked the world.

sand, men, women and children had been killed. Some people would later maintain that far more than one thousand had died that night. Several dozen soldiers who were killed by protesters were instantly praised as being martyrs by government propagandists. The world was in shock.

All over Beijing and in many other cities

throughout China the army also moved in and killed. This had happened before in China—many, many times before. But this time was different. This time the event was seen all over the world, on television, on radio. The government could not hide what it had done, except—ironically—from its own people. The blood was quickly washed from Tiananmen Square. The bodies were burned and buried in mass graves. Suspected protesters were arrested or went into hiding. Within hours, the Chinese government was proclaiming that it had "put down a counter-revolutionary rebellion" started by "an extremely small handful of people." They applauded the army for their "patriot zeal" and pinned medals on the generals. Zhao Ziyang was put under arrest and relieved of his duties. The government tried to convince the international press that what they had seen on television hadn't really happened.

But nothing the government did convinced anyone. The violent images remained on videotape, in everyone's memory. Perhaps the most powerful of these images was the film taken early on the morning after the massacre. A single Chinese student stood in front of a line of tanks, refusing to move.

The world's response was immediate and condemning. Governments recalled their ambassadors and their money from China. Foreign businesses abandoned their offices in China; most have not returned. Tourists who had flocked to China in large numbers suddenly stopped coming. More than 30,000 Chinese students studying abroad refused to return to China. The U.S. government extended the visas of students studying in this country.

What Of Tomorrow?

Today, the consequences of the Chinese government's decision to crush the democracy movement are clear. There has been a sudden, crippling drop in China's economy. The government has had only limited success in convincing foreign business to return. The withdrawal of foreign trade, the closing of universities, and the return of harsh martial law has pushed China into a former, darker era.

Li Peng is now premier, though Deng Xiaoping remains the power behind the throne. Again and again, Li has emphasized the need for a "dictatorship of the proletariat." The military and police have been strengthened, and universities must now emphasize "education in Marxist-Leninism and Mao." Primary and middle schools, proclaim Li, must "educate pupils in ways appropriate to their age levels, in patriotism, collectivism, socialism, communism..." The Party is trying to exercise a new "guidance" over the people, which means once again supervising every aspect of their daily lives.

The government has said more than a few times that the events in Eastern Europe and the Soviet Union would have no effect on China, that "socialism" would continue there. Despite this, Chinese officials have tried to win back world business and goodwill. They do not seem to understand that it is impossible to have a free market economy—or the support of the free world—without giving greater individual freedom to their own people.

Deng Xiaoping, now in his eighties, stepped down from his position as Chinese leader and formally announced that Jiang Zemin would become his successor. Jiang, like Li Peng, is a political conservative who believes in dictatorship and a strong military. He too sees democracy as the enemy.

The results of this sudden, brutal return to earlier political policies does not come at a good time for China. The World Bank, which once provided billions of dollars to help China, has cancelled future loans and refuses to do any more business with China's rulers.

The residents of Hong Kong, a British-governed territory scheduled to rejoin China in 1997, protested the crackdown. Many have requested permission to move to Great Britain to

Living In China

- *October 1, 1989 marked the 40th anniversary of the People's Republic of China.*

- *The Chinese language is made up of 140,000 characters—far more complex than our own 26-character alphabet.*

- *Wushu is the correct term for Kungfu. The ancient art goes back to the 6th century B.C. Shaolin monks patterned wushu after the movements of wild animals.*

- *Pool—or billiards—is a popular game in China, so much so that tables are set up along roadsides for play.*

- *In Yunnan, women of the Naxi tribe used to be dominant—men would cook and women would rule the roost and inherit all the property. The Naxi tribe barely exists today.*

- *Acupuncture has been practiced in China for nearly 2,500 years.*

escape communism.

Relations between China and the United States have soured. Relations with the rest of Europe and most of the Third World are no better. At present, China can hardly be called a world partner.

It is hard to predict what the future has in store for China. The current dictatorship will not give up power without bloodshed, and there has already been too much blood spilled. Without money or assistance from the outside world, many of the reforms Deng tried to begin are sure

to fail. The economy, never very healthy, is in serious trouble. The people are unhappy. Hatred and suspicion of the government and its policies are openly discussed by the Chinese in many parts of the country.

Many experts believe China must change when Deng dies, but others think that the Communist regime will keep itself in power for a long time to come. If the government succeeds in its plan, it will isolate China completely from other nations. As the rest of the world grows more prosperous, China is destined to fall further and further behind. The world will simply pass them by. If this happens, the Chinese will remain a third world country. With a limited amount of productive land supporting an unlimited population, China's people will do what they have had to do so many times before—suffer and starve.

In 1972, Richard Nixon became the first American president to visit China. His walk along the Great Wall marked a new era in U.S. diplomatic relations with the world's largest Communist nation. Today, relations are strained as a result of the Chinese government's response to the rebellion at Tiananmen Square.

Glossary

BRIGADE. A subunit of the old style commune. Brigades were comprised of many people.

CADRE. Person or group who holds any responsible position in either the government or the party.

COMMUNE. The largest unit in the rural areas from 1958 to 1985 when they were replaced by townships. These units had political, economic and governmental control over a group of people living in a single area. All land within the commune area, all products grown by the commune workers, and all services provided by commune personnel were owned by the commune on behalf of the state.

COMMUNISM. A system derived by Karl Marx and Friedrich Engels, two German philosophers. It calls for the overthrow of the rich and middle class by the workers. While this word is often used to describe both Russia and China, neither country practices true communism, which so far has proved unworkable. The system of government really practiced by both countries is a form of dictatorship sometimes referred to as totalitarianism, where a small group of people control every aspect of public and private life.

CONFUCIANISM. A system of philosophy first described by Confucius around 550 B.C. This philosophy emphasized the importance of relationships, especially family ties, in which loyalty and fidelity were considered the greatest virtues. Only those men who were gentlemanly and superior should be rulers, said Confucius, and life should be led ethically no matter who you were.

FOUR MODERNIZATIONS. The development aimed at turning China around by the year 2000. Its major targets are agriculture, industry, science and technology, and national defense. First launched by Zhou Enlai, it became the official party line under Deng Xiaoping.

LONG MARCH. The 12,500-kilometer march made by the Red Army during the Communist revolution. Began in October 1934 in Jiangxi Province and ended in October 1935 in Shaanxi Province. Some 100,000 persons left the communist base area in Jiangxi, but only about 28,000 arrived in Yan'an, Chinese Communist Party headquarters for the next decade. It was during the Long March that Mao Zedong gained leadership of the party.

MARXIST-LENINISM. The combining of the political beliefs of two men, the German philosopher Karl Marx and the founder of the Soviet Union, V.I. Lenin. It proposes overthrow of the rich and middle class everywhere by the workers and the establishment of a "workers paradise" where all men are equal. But while Marx believed such a process would occur naturally over time, Lenin's version called for violent revolution.

PINYIN. The modern English spellings of Chinese names as adopted by China in 1979. The old method was called the Wade-Giles romanization. This means that names like Mao Tse-tung in the Wade-Giles system now become Mao Zedong in the Pinyin system, and Teng Hsiao-p'ing become Deng Xiaoping. Many city names have also changed as well;

for example, Canton is now Guangzhou.

Of course, romanization cannot success-
fully translate Chinese which depends on pitch
as much as pronunciation to tell the listener
the meaning. For example, the word *ma* can
have four distinctly different meanings,
depending on the pitch of the voice.

PUTONGHUA. The common spoken language;
also called *guoyu*. Putonghua is based on the
northern dialect (Mandarin), and uses Beijing
pronunciations as its standard.

RED BOOK. The sayings and writings of Mao
Zedong as written in a red-covered book.
Hundreds of millions of copies are in print.

REVISIONISM. A term used by Communists to
mean any straying from the path of "true
communism." What this often means is any
action that disagrees with the party in power.

Bibliography

China, the land, the cities, the people, the culture, the present, Exeter Press, 1985

Clayre, Alasdair. *The Heart of the Dragon*, Houghton-Mifflin, 1985

Fairbank, John K. and Edwin O. Reischauer. *East Asia: the GreatTradition*. Houghton-Mifflin, 1960

Fairbank, John K., Edwin O. Reischauer and Albert M. Craig. *East Asia: the Modern Transformation*. Houghton-Mifflin, 1965

Malloy, Ruth Lor. *Fielding's People's Republic of China. 1988*. Fielding Travel Books, 1988

Nation, Richard. "The Tactics of Terror." *The Spectator.* June 17, 1989, vol. 262

Schurmann, Franz and Orville Schell. *Communist China.* Vintage Book, 1967

Simpson, John. "Tiananmen Square." *Granta Magazine.* Autumn, 1989, vol. 28, Penguin Press

Wedeman, Andrew Hall. *The East Wind Subsides.* Washington Institute Book, 1987

Worden, Robert L. and Andrea M. Savada, etc. (ed.) *China, a Country Study.* United States Government. 1988

Index

Picture Credits